The Dark Side of Photography

The Dark Side of Photography

Thomas Roth Jr.

The Dark Side of Photography

And How to See the Light

Missing Toe Publishing
Chester, SC USA

Contents

Why You Should Read this Book

You are a unique photographer, and you want your images to show it. You are a creative person with a need for expression. You have a desire to create and sell more images. If any of this describes you, then you need to read this book.

In this book <u>The Dark Side of Photography and How to find the Light</u>, I discuss the negative emotions that can affect the quality of your work, or stop it all together. I call these negative emotions the "dark side." I define what the dark side is, and its effect on you can be. I define three areas that the dark side tends to target. I also discuss how to recognize when you are slipping into the dark side, and how to stop or reverse your course.

How to find the light offers suggestions on ways to overcome the dark side. I define what the "light "is, and why we want to find it. The light is what all creative people strive to attain. I this book I discuss ways to achieve the light in your life.

WARNING!!

If you think you do not need to read this book, then you may already be slipping to the DARK SIDE!

Introduction

I love photography. I really do. I love every-thing about the craft. I love reading about photog-raphers, and their work. I love sorting out the days shots. I love writing about the photos I make. I really get excited and love making a sale. I love the prepara-tion that it takes to have a great day shooting images. I love sitting at the computer and key wording those shots. There really isn't anything that I don't enjoy about the photography craft and business.

My love of the photography business started some forty years ago. Things were much different in the pre digital days. The thrill of receiving a stack of boxes with slides in them for me to edit, and label was always one of the most enjoyable parts of my day. Nothing could beat the excitement of going to the lab and getting the first sight of a well printed 16x20 print. I could go on about film and digital and their differences, but that's only a very small change that the digital word has created. The real change, the one that has made the biggest difference is the speed in which the world can now communicate.

The United States post office has been and still does a very good job of getting documents and products to my clients. Sometimes I just have to have an actual physical product to the client for their approval, but today, most of my work can be done through the internet. The speed in which I can receive feedback or even a payment is now minutes instead of days. This speed has provided a new thrill, and creates great excitement. My love of photography has now been given a new drug, a very addictive one, and I thoroughly enjoy it.

A love of photography like mine and yours can be enjoyable and profitable, but there is also a "dark side' to this love affair. There is a dark side of photography that nobody seems to want to discuss. This dark side of photography can push your love of the craft to its' very limits. There is a negative side of photography that can stop a photographer dead in their tracks, and destroy any hopes of being creative. I know, I've been there, and I'll bet you have to.

That's why I have written this book; to help those who come after me, better deal with those negative emotions. We all are human and experience negative emotions, and maybe what I talk about can smooth out the rough spots.

The Dark Side

What is the dark side

What is the "dark side?" How do we get to the "dark side?" What happens to us when enter into the "dark side?" Where is the "dark side?" Do we even know when we have entered the "dark side?" This is what the book is all about. I will attempt to inform, identify, caution, and offer suggestion to avoid the "dark side" of photography.

The dark side of photography is those thoughts and emotions that can ruin any chances of being not only a professional photographer, but also the ability to make great images. I call these negative emotions the dark side of photography. No one is immune for falling to the dark side. It's easy to do, and can be comfortable.

Being comfortable is where the real danger is because the more comfortable you are the more you like it and remain in the comfort of the dark side. The dark side can be very appealing. Everyone enjoys being comfortable.

Tomorrow is the dark side's best friend. Tomorrow will always be a better day when dealing with the dark side of photography. In fact the dark side cannot exist without tomorrow. The sun will always rise tomorrow and the dark side of photography will never let you forget this.

The dark side of photography does not care about your money. The dark side will always keep you broke. The dark side wants you to be comfortable, while at the same time it takes your money. Many times you realize that your money is being taken from you but, the dark side keeps you so comfortable that you don't even care. If you have gone this far into the dark side it's time to reach out for help. This is the painful part of the dark side.

The dark side can be very creative in tricking you into believing that you are comfortable. The dark side will lie to you in a heartbeat. At the same time that the dark side is lying to you the dark side will hit you between the eyes with the truth.

The dark side likes to keep you confused. The more confused you become the more powerful the dark side will become. Confusion can keep you locked in a downward turn towards the dark side.

One of the purposes of this book is to help you avoid the dangers of the dark side. There are ways to stop the progression of the dark side. To stop the dark side from getting to you, one must know the signs that indicate the dark side is near. You don't have to be uncomfortable to beat the dark side. You will have to make some sacrifices and exercise a little will power to keep the dark side at bay.

I have found that almost all of my encounters with the dark side have come in three areas: 1-Equipment 2-Talent 3-Success. Each area has its' own indicators of slipping into the dark side. Before you can have a solution to a problem you first identify the problems and their sources. Let's take a look at each the three areas and examine the problems and the source.

Equipment

I love photography equipment. Buying a new camera is one of the biggest thrills I can think of. When I switched over from film to digital I first researched what manufacturer to build my system on. Once that decision was made I then researched the model that I could afford. With the vast resources of the internet I searched for the best price from a reputable company and made my purchase.

When my purchase arrived I enjoyed the process of unpacking the contents. The smell of new electronics, the crispness of the owner's manual, and the joy of charging the batteries, could entertain me for hours. There are very few joys in the world as wonderful as the arrival of new equipment. (In my opinion) The whole process of buying and receiving a new piece of equipment can be intoxicating, and addictive. This is when the dark side of photography slips in.

A lust for new equipment can ruin you if you are not very careful. The desire to always have the next new gadget or software can stop you in your creative tracks. The desire for new equipment can keep you from ever getting out of the gate. How could

something as the purchase of new gear be so dangerous?

There are several reasons that equipment can
be so dangerous and lead to the dark side. The first
way that the purchase of new equipment can lead
to the dark side is that, if you are always looking at
new gear, how can you master the gear you already
have. This may not hold true so much as with lenses
and filters, but is certainly true of software and camera bodies. It takes time and more time to become
proficient at using the tools of our craft. The photographers that produce the top selling photography are
masters with their tools.

Another reason that gear can lead to the dark
side is a double edge sword. Not having the gear that
you need to produce a great shot, and not having
the money to buy the gear to take that great shot.
The dark side has surely entered into your life when
you believe that you can only make great shots if you
have the money to purchase all the latest gear.

Depression from gear will stop any creative
endeavors that the photographer had dreamed of.
When you suffer depression from lack of equipment
it is hard to even get out of the house. Depression
from lack of equipment will not allow you to think
creatively because you cannot focus on what you do
have. Suffering from lack of equipment always provides a great excuse of why you didn't get the shot.

Lust for new equipment that you cannot afford will keep you in the poor house. This is the dark side that does not care about your money. The dark side of photography that keeps you trapped is in a never ending battle with your money, and a lust for new equipment feeds the enemy. A lack of money to buy the latest equipment is not the problem but a symptom of the real problem. Nothing can be more painful that wanting something you cannot afford.

It is easy to understand these symptoms of falling into the dark side, but there is still another danger that equipment may bring. This danger is not as easy to spot as some of the other dangers, but just as every bit as deadly in your creative pursuits. Too much equipment!

Our equipment captivates us. We spend too much of time playing with every lens, filter, and flash that we can afford to bring. How many times have we missed the action, or the perfect moment because we were too busy changing this or that. Having lots of equipment can be fun, but it can also cause you to miss out of some of the best images.

Equipment can bring a photographer to dark side by spending too much time on the controls. Yes, f stops, shutter speeds, and aperture settings are important, but getting the shot is more important. Todays' electronic cameras offer more control over the image than ever before, and it is very easy to get caught in all the adjustments that you can make. Remember you here to make images not play with the controls. Keep the use of adjustments limited and you can avoid the "dark side."

The last word on the danger of your equipment can pose to your creativity, and that is limiting the use of viewing when making images. The instant feedback from making an image is a great tool when used correctly. Use the LCD screen to check exposure and clarity, but not for editing. If you are busy editing, then how can you be with your subject.

Anyone can slip into equipment depression, it's easy to do. It feels good to buy a new piece of gear. It's fun to have choices in our camera bag. Having, buying, and using equipment is part of why I love photography so much, but the dangers of equipment depression are always present.

The dark side and talent go hand in hand. Before we can discuss the dark side of photography and talent, we must first define what talent is.

The definition of talent according to dictionary.com is 1-a special **natural** ability or aptitude, and 2-a capacity for achievement or success. The definition for our discussion is the photographer that consistently brings home spectacular photos. These photographers visit all the same places that everyone else does and still brings home unique and wonderful images. The photography magazines are full of theses photographers.

Just as with equipment the real culprit here is depression. Nothing is more depressing to go with other photographers to a beautiful location and your shots are not is cool as some of the other photographers. The brain of the photographers' first thoughts is "I'm just not as talented as those other guys", and then the excuses start to really come forward. The photographer has thoughts like, they (other photographers) have been photographing longer then I have. They have been there before, and the killer we discussed earlier, they have better equipment then I do. If the photographer believes any of these statements to be true, then depression steps in.

If we stick to the second definition of talent as ones capacity for achievement and success then we can see that everyone has such capacity. This can be a double edge sword for the photographer. The fact that we all have the capacity for achievement is great reason to have hope and keep the struggle towards that goal alive. The downside is if we all have the capacity for achievement, then I must be a failure because I have not experienced such achievement.

Talent is subjective, and that is why it can so dangerous for the photographer. There are many areas of photography. For some reason us photographer creative types think that we must be talented in all areas. As photographers we tend to beat ourselves up because we cannot make a wonderful portrait, yet we can create incredible composite images. We judge ourselves on the lack of talent to produce the portrait.

Talent is our perception of what other people think of our images. The dark side will amplify any and all negative comments to prove to your inner self that you have no talent. The dark side does not believe that you have any talent. The dark side wants you to believe your chances for achievement are always just out of reach.

Success and Achievement

The dark side loves losers! One of the quickest ways to the dark side is to feel sorry for yourself when you do not succeed. Self-pity is one of the strongest tools of the dark side. Sure, we all have heard not to allow ourselves to wallow in pity, but it is different for us creative types.

When the show the next great American artist was on the air, the contestants (artists) would be critiqued by a panel of gallery owners and famous artists. It did not seem to matter if the critique was positive or negative; some contestants broke down into tears. It's never easy to sit and listen to someone critique your work and negative reviews can send you reeling towards the dark side.

A negative critique is not the only way that achievement give send you to the dark side. Sometimes too much success can send us deep into the dark side. With too much success the mind begins to believe that there is no reason to continue. In your mind you have reached a level of success and there just can't be any reason to create; besides someone else needs to win. When you begin to think like this, then get some batteries for your TV remote. The dark side has entered into your life.

Chasing success can lead to feeling of jealousy. The dark side and jealousy go hand in hand. Remember that the darks side loves to remind you that you are not very talented, and you don't have the right gear. The dark side loves for you to be jealous of another's success. If you feel yourself being a little envious of another's accomplishment, then you are very close to the dark side.

Summary

There is a negative emotional side to photography, just as there is with many aspects of life. I refer to these negative emotions as the "dark side" of photography. These negative emotions or the dark side can lead to a path of destruction for the photographer that wants to be creative. I most cases I can trace the entry into dark side to one of three areas. These areas are Equipment and Gear, Talent, and Success.

"I think everybody should get rich and famous, and do everything they ever dreamed of so they can see that it's not the answer."

Actor Jim Carrey

The Dark Side of Photography

How to find the light

What is the Light

The light that I am referring to is not the light used to make photographs. The light I am talking about is the light that lets you flow with creativity. The light I am talking about is a feeling not a physical attribute. The light is a feeling that keeps you excited, and gets you out of bed in the morning.

Why do we want to find the light

Photography can be a lonely job. Many of us are self-employed. Many of us spend hours alone in the field or in front of a computer. For many of us the entire process of survival rest on our shoulders. Working alone isn't necessarily a bad thing. Many photographers enjoy this alone time.

Alone with yourself is when the dark side likes to work, and that is the reason you need to find the light. The light can save you from yourself. Creativity can get you started on a project, but the light keeps you fired up and out there working. When creativity and the light mesh together magic happens. Finding the light can catapult or start your photography career.

The light will help you with your money. The light cares about you money, unlike the dark side which likes to keep you broke. When you find the light, it can help you make more money, and better manage the money you make.

Finding the light will improve your relationships with others. The light will help you lead a balanced life. A balanced life includes healthy relationships with others and yourself.

To put it as simply as possible, the light will make your life better and more fun.

With so much pressure from the dark side, it is amazing that anyone chooses photography as hobby, let alone a profession. And if you a human you will most likely fall prey to the dark side at some time during your photographic journey. Do not worry! That is what this book is all about: to inform you of what the dark side is and how to avoid falling to its commands. There is hope and it is easy.

We have covered what the dark side is. We have decided that there are three areas that can affect we view ourselves with our photographs. These three areas are gear, talent, and accomplishment. We have discussed how the dark side uses gear, talent, and accomplishment against us. We know that the dark side can cripple any chance of being creative with photography. So what are you to do?

Just as there are many ways to enter the dark side, there are just as many ways to defend you from the dark side. Let's take a look at some of those methods to combat the dark side.

Learn to catch yourself before It's Too Late

By understanding how the dark side works, we can have a plan that can prevent or reverse the damages of the dark side. We know that the dark side likes to attack our weakness. So, step one is to learn when the dark side is beginning to attack. Most of the time the dark side will begin its attack with a simple excuse, and build from there until you are stuck on the couch watching Jerry Springer. Here is the tricky part: the excuse may be valid.

Define what achievement and success is for you.

Success is a very subjective. Each person must define what success is for them and only themselves. The definition for success is different for me then it is for you. If you do not have a definition for achievement and success, then the dark side is just sitting and waiting for you to come on over. When you are sure what success and achievement means to you. The dark side has a very difficult time in entering into your life.

Not all excuses are a lie. It may be very true that the close-up that you wanted to get is impossible, so you give up on making close-ups. It may be very true that you lacked the right gear to capture the subject. Here is the danger with this kind of excuse; you are so convinced that you don't have the right gear that you don't even attempt to make an image. When you are having this kind of thought you are very close to the dark side.

To make matters worse your friend was photographing the same subject with the same gear, and produced a wonderful close-up of the subject. A week later you see that your friend won a contest with that same close-up shot. You have just experienced a triple dark side whammy. You did not have the right gear, your friend was more talented, and his accomplishment was just lucky. Be very careful when you experience thoughts like these; you are very close to the dark side.

When you find yourself thinking in terms of excuse and not possibilities you are entering into the dark side of photography. If you can catch yourself early on in the excuse making process then you can quickly squash those negative producing feelings. The fastest way to erase those feelings is to go back to the beginning.

How to return to the light

Return to the Beginning

When I was thirteen I became attracted to photography. I will never forget the amazement I experienced when I saw my first image appear like magic in a tray of developer perched on the sink in the family bathroom. When I find myself making excuses, I remind myself of the amazement of those first darkroom days. If you find yourself making excuses, then go back to beginning when you were first attracted to photography.

Set Goals

Goal setting and photography go hand in hand. If you find yourself making excuses, then now is the perfect time to set goals. By setting goal you can keep your mind focused on what is important and the excuses become challenges. Goal setting can keep you positive when everything seems to be heading in the wrong direction. There are thousands of books on goal setting and if you don't have one then you need to get a book on goal setting, and get some photography goals set.

Become Project Orientated.

When you focused on a project, it is much the same as goal. You can stay focused because you there is an end to project. The biggest difference between a goal and a project is that a project may be one of your goals. A project may contain many goals to complete the project, and may require some non-photographic skills. A project may be for personal reasons or one that has been assigned to you by a client.

Practice Makes Perfect

Practice of your photography skills should always be one of your goals. The good thing about practicing is that you are allowed to make mistakes. It is the mistakes that we learn how to do the job better. Just don't let the excuses in your mind stop you from practicing. If you don't have that macro lens that could make the job easier, then come up other ways to shoot the subject that is visually interesting.

Learn to Think in Concepts

When you think in terms of concepts instead of single images, then you can choose which photos you will include and which will not be included. Having more than one image in a concept allows you more freedom to make mistakes. A concept can be easier on the brain, because you can make many images that may convey the concept. The brain enjoys the flow from one thought to another, it is the flow of these thoughts that can help produce great images of the concept that you are trying to convey.

Find Some Inspirational material

This may seem obvious, but it is one of the quickest ways to overcome the depression that can accompany the dark side. Magazines are a great place to get inspired. The reason that magazines are a great resource is that there is a magazine to fit every ones taste. Look for the subjects that you are interested in and look at the photography in those publications. Not ever photograph in the magazine is a stellar image, but you can learn from the not so good images just as much as you can learn from those spectacular images.

A good book can help beat the dark side also. When you read a good book it expands your mind. When you expand your mind you are open to more and better ideas. With a mind full of new ideas you can easily push away the effects of the dark side. The book you chose does not have to be about photography or photographers; they can be on any subject that excites you. The key purpose is to find inspirational material that replaces your excuses with positive new goals that cause excitement to build in yourself. With your new found excitement, you can now go and create great images.

Clean your Equipment

Cleaning your equipment can be a big stress reliever. There is something about knowing that your equipment is clean and memory cards formatted and ready to go, that can get you off the couch and into the field shooting photos. Sometimes cleaning your equipment can help clear your mind. With a clear mind you can then set those goals. With a clear mind mistakes become more manageable. With a clear mind you can look objectively at your subject. Cleaning your equipment and formatting those memory cards just may be the answer to keep you from going to the dark side.

Sleep

As simple as this may sound sometimes the answer is to get a good night's sleep, and start fresh the next day. There are alternatives to sleep such as taking a walk. Sometimes the answer to a problem or an excuse can only happen when you step away for a while.

Don't be a perfectionist

We all want to create the perfect image. There is nothing wrong for wanting to the best that you possibly can, but sometimes perfection is just not going to happen. There limits to everything we do and we must come to terms with that fact. Every image we create cannot be perfect, but it can be darn good.

Failure is never finial

The only way to really lose is to quit. When you treat every experience as a tool for learning, then each failure is a stepping stone towards the next goal. If you give up and quit, then you have not only slipped over to the dark side, the dark side has won.

Use the force of momentum

One of the best tools to defend your-self from entering the dark side is the use of momentum. Momentum occurs when you have started and are excited about its completion. When you come close to the finish of one project pick another of your goals and keep the momentum going. The dark side has little power over a goal setter with momentum.

Accept success with gratitude

We all love to win. Being recognized for excellence among your peers is one of the honors anyone can receive. To keep yourself from slipping over to the dark side accept your award with thankfulness. Do not let your-self become too proud, and remain humble. When in doubt remember the phrase, "to those with gratitude more will be given, and to those without gratitude even the little they have will be taken away." Always be thankful for you achievement, and be thankful for any and all that have helped you along the way.

Never stop learning

The dark side cannot survive in a person that is always learning. Learn to love to learn. The first place to start is with the industry that you are involved in. The internet provides a vast array of knowledge for anyone to learn. Do not become too one sided; continuing learning in others areas of your life. A well balanced approach is best.

Turn failures into success

The always learning photographer knows there is no such thing as failure. Every critique, comment, or missed sale is a learning experience. From any experience, take away the good and learn from the bad. Many, many times I have heard that a great accomplishment only became possible because of the failure before the achievement. This goes along with failure is never finial.

Don't judge your-self on what you cannot do.

Ii's easy to get down on your-self when you concentrate on the things you have a difficult time with. Yes, you need to practice on those areas you have a difficult time with, but remember that is just what it is, practice. When you practice you are allowed to screw things up. Don't judge yourself on your practice photos.

Become a problem solver

Problem solvers can always find a job. Think in terms of solutions. It is very difficult for the dark side to attack when you are solving a problem.

What will not save you from the dark side?

We have discussed ways to find the light, but I need to mention that there ways that will keep you from finding the light.

Drugs and Alcohol

This may seem obvious but, two of the most powerful tools of the dark side are drugs (this includes alcohol), and money. You cannot find the light with drugs and alcohol; many have tried, and ended up in total darkness. There is nothing wrong with taking a break and having a drink, but this will prolong any chance of reaching the light. It is very difficult to be the party person, and still achieve a level of creativity needed to complete in this world. This is true for all professions. The dark side will constantly remind you, "that all work and no play make Jack a dull boy." This may be true, but be very careful when thinking like this.

More Money

If you think you lack money to be creative, then money is not your problem. There are hundreds if not thousands of books written on money, and how to obtain and save it. If you feel that money is your problem then you should get a book or two and learn about money. You will learn that the lack of money is not your problem but it is your attitude about money that matters most.

There are thousands of people that buy lots of gear. They have all the coolest equipment that money can buy, but they rarely capture a decent image. All the money in the world will not help them capture a better image then a photographer that has found the light.

Money can help you become a better photographer, if spent wisely. Education is one of the areas that money can help, but even here there is a danger to rely too much on the next big thing. Money cannot replace doing!

To sum it all up, drugs, alcohol, and money in most cases will not get you closer to finding the light.

Summary on Light

We know that there are negative emotions that hinder creativity, and refer to these emotions as the dark side. Light can counter the dark side. Emotions that create light in our lives are referred to as light. If we can recognize that we a falling towards the dark side, then we can use different tools to counter the negative emotions. We can find the light, and create spectacular images.

The Dark Side of Photography